U.S. DOT FY 2012 Research, Development and Technology Budget

Meeting with Staff from the Technology & Innovation Subcommittee

March 23, 2011

U.S. Department of Transportation

Research and Innovative Technology Administration

AGENDA

Welcome by Administrator Appel	10:00
Federal Motor Carrier Safety Administration (FMCSA) Overview	10:05
National Highway Transportation Safety Administration (NHTSA) Overview	10:15
Federal Railroad Administration (FRA) Overview	10:25
Federal Transit Administration (FTA) Overview	10:35
Federal Highway Administration (FHWA) Overview	10:45
Research and Innovative Technology Administration (RITA) Overview	10:55
Discussion	11:05

Table of Contents

United States Department of Transportation Surface Transportation FY2012 Research, Development, and Technology (RD&T) Budget

Introduction

The U.S. Department of Transportation's (U.S. DOT's) FY2012 Research, Development and Technology (RD&T) budget related to surface transportation reflects the Department's strategic goals to improve safety, ensure that transportation assets are maintained in a state of good repair, work to achieve environmental sustainability, foster livable communities, and support the Nation's long-term economic competiveness.. Achieving these goals will transform our transportation infrastructure into a truly multimodal integrated system that provides the traveling public and U.S. businesses with safe, convenient, affordable and environmentally sustainable transportation choices.

U.S. DOT's RD&T efforts span all modes of transportation, enabling improvements to the Nation's transportation system and supporting data-driven decision-making about national priorities. U.S. DOT's Research and Innovative Technology Administration (RITA) coordinates the RD&T Planning Council which is composed of the heads of the operating administrations, and other senior DOT leaders. The RD&T Planning Team includes the operating administrations' Associate Administrators for RD&T.

Through the Council and Team, the U.S. DOT takes a department-wide, systems-level view of the multimodal transportation system, addresses research areas that go beyond a modal-oriented and modal-funded perspective, and ensures that RD&T resources are invested wisely to achieve measurable improvements in our Nation's transportation system. The Council and Team, led by the Research and Innovative Technology Administration (RITA), drive an ongoing coordination process involving all U.S. DOT operating administrations and the Office of the Secretary. This process incorporates multiyear strategic planning, annual program planning, and budget and performance planning across DOT, as well as the unique mission requirements of U.S. DOT's operating administrations. The result is cross-modal planning and collaboration of RD&T at the highest levels of U.S. DOT.

Transportation RD&T has the potential to unlock transformative solutions that can may lead to dramatic improvements in our Nation's transportation systems. Federal investment in transportation RD&T has led to the development of new materials, innovative production methods, and powerful design and planning tools. It has provided decision makers with information and knowledge to make better decisions, and operators with technologies and tools to solve problems.

The organization of the U.S. DOT into operating administrations, each with its own statutory requirements and missions, makes collaborative cross-modal research challenging. Federal policies for surface transportation, aviation, and passenger rail are established through separate legislation and draw funding from separate sources. Many operating administrations, for example, must devote substantial portions of their RD&T budgets to research supporting their internal regulatory rulemaking activities. While operating administrations are interested in addressing cross-modal issues, they have limited flexibility to allocate resources to such research.

U.S. DOT engages in cooperative and joint research with stakeholders and partners across the transportation sector, including other Federal agencies, State and local agencies, academia, industry, and not-for-profit institutions, such as the American Association of State Highway and Transportation Officials (AASHTO), the Transportation Research Board (TRB), and the American Public Transportation Association (APTA). U.S. DOT will continue to consult and coordinate with transportation research partners such as the Transportation Research Board, State and local governments, academic institutions, transportation industry, and the general public to promote an integrated and effective transportation system, leveraging all modal resources.

Federal Motor Carrier Safety Administration (FMCSA)

Research and Technology Program

The FMCSA Research and Technology (R&T) program request is $11.6 million in FY 2012. This supports FMCSA's safety mission through the development of future agency regulations, programs, methodologies, ideas, and tools to advance CMV safety to improve safety. R&T funding supports diverse set of Agency's offices and priorities including: research to produce safer drivers via naturalistic driving, onboard monitoring, and driver fatigue programs; Policy Development and Rulemaking, examples include driver distraction, hours of service and entry level training; the Agency's Enforcement Activities including Hazardous Materials and Motorcoach research and the Agency's Congressionally-mandated Small Business Innovative Research (SBIR) Program. The current budget was built via annual call for research proposals; the final proposals will be vetted and ranked by the Research Executive Board (REB). Each year the R&T Program is comprised of new starts and continuation projects. With the requested funds the following studies will be funded:

R&T PROGRAM NAME: *Produce Safer Drivers: $4.2M*

- **Annual Driver Survey.** To obtain an understanding of the impact of changes in the commercial driver workforce to ensure safety and well-being of its members. The results will be used to develop and evaluate rules, regulations, policies, and enforcement activities for the motor carrier industry.
- **CDL Endorsement for Fuel-Saving Driving.** Draft a consensus-based standard for fuel-savings driving techniques training. Evaluate the results of drivers trained under such a standard against other drivers. Develop approaches to certifying completion of this training as part of a commercial driver's license (CDL).
- **Driver Distraction—Eye Glance Analysis: An Evaluation of the Risks Posed by Electronic Devices.** Complete an in-depth study of eye glance behavior as it relates to crash risk. Eye glance behavior is of fundamental importance to gain a more detailed understanding of how eye movements are associated with crash risk.
- **Effects of Detention Times on CMV Driver Fatigue.** The purpose of this research is to better understand the nature of the problem of detention or waiting times in the CMV industry.
- **Expert Panel Report Review of Hours of Service for Passenger Carrier Operations.** The objective of this project is to convene an expert panel to review the research and make recommendations regarding changes to passenger carrier hours of service (HOS) regulations.

- **Impact of Driver Compensation Systems on CMV Safety.** The objective of this study is to examine the impact of driver compensation (i.e., pay per mile or pay by the hour) on CMV safety.

- **Individualized Fatigue Risk Management in Trucking Operations.** The objective of this project is to develop an individualized FMP model that takes into account individual differences and driving performance. This model will be developed into a tool that could be commercialized for use by the motor carrier industry for scheduling CMV drivers.

- **North American Fatigue Management Program (Phase IV).** The objective of this study is develop materials, guidelines, standards and processes necessary for a motor carrier to prepare for and implement a comprehensive and effective fatigue management program (FMP).

- **Onboard Monitoring Field Operational Test: 270 Truck Study.** The objective of the OBMS program is to determine whether on-board monitoring will reduce at-risk behavior among commercial drivers and improve driver safety performance. This project will execute a Field Operation Test (FOT) of an onboard monitoring suite with at three commercial vehicle fleets that are representative of the trucking industry. Across these fleets, 270 OBMS devices will be used and instrumented on trucks.

- **Performance-Based Testing of Driver Skills/Capabilities.** The objective of this research is to determine the extent to which older CMV drivers pose a safety risk. This research is needed to support future rulemaking aimed at developing performance-base testing and determining the cost and safety benefits of such a program.

- **Random Roadside Drug Testing Analysis.** The objective is to develop a voluntary random roadside drug testing survey that tests for the same DOT requirements in order to more accurately measure the current baseline level of illegal drug usage by CMV drivers, and to measure the future effectiveness of FMCSA's drug and alcohol program initiatives.

- **Safety Data Risk Study (Phase III).** The objective of this study is to investigate the feasibility of identifying CMV driver factors that increase the risk of large truck crashes.

- **Study of Alternative Methods to Reduce Driver Exposure to Diesel Exhaust PM2.5.** This study will investigate alternatives to reduce emission that enter a truck cab thereby improving air quality that driver are exposed to while sleeping in a sleeper berth

- **Study of Individual Driver Factors that make them Vulnerable to Fatigue.** The objective of this research is to determine if it is possible to identify individuals who may be vulnerable to fatigue and provide set of best practices for motor carriers aim at reducing driver fatigue by matching driver fatigue vulnerability to work schedules.

- **Update to the Model Training Curriculum for Motorcoach Drivers.** This research will update the model curriculum for training motorcoach drivers by obtaining and incorporating the necessary information.
- **Wireless Roadside Inspection Field Operational Test (Phase III).** To improve highway safety through the dramatic increase of roadside safety inspections of heavy trucks and buses and their drivers enabled by wireless communications between vehicles and inspectors at highway.

RD&T PROGRAM NAME: *Improve Safety of CMVs: $1.9M*

- **CMV/Train Collision Avoidance.** To develop a system for avoiding/minimizing a collision between a commercial vehicle and a train at a highway-railroad grade crossing.
- **Enhanced Rear Signaling Field Operational Test.** The countermeasures developed in this project will be field tested on a fleet of heavy trucks to determine their potential to reduce rear end crashes involving heavy trucks.
- **FMCSA Advanced System Testing Data Acquisition System on the Highways (FAST DASH) Program.** The objective of the FAST DASH (FMCSA's Advanced System Testing program utilizing a Data Acquisition System Highway) is to conduct a fast turn-around and independent evaluation of promising safety technologies aimed at commercial vehicle operations.

R&T PROGRAM NAME: *Produce Safer Carriers: $1.1M*

- **Analysis of the Effectiveness of the FMCSA CSA 2010 Training Program.** To analyze the effectiveness of FMCSA's CSA2010 Training Program in enhancing the FMCSA workforce's knowledge and ability to conduct enforcement and compliance reviews to improve commercial motor vehicle safety.
- **Hazardous Materials Navigation Safety and Security System.** To develop a low-cost hazardous materials (HM) navigation system for motor carriers and drivers that take into account HM routing based on safety and security concerns.
- **Research to Support FMCSA Rulemaking Activities. The objective of this activity is t**o fund an Indefinite Delivery Indefinite Quantity (IDIQ) contract for research to support FMCSA's rulemaking activities.

R&T PROGRAM NAME: *Information-Based Initiatives: $0.5M*

- **National CVISN Deployment Program.** The objective of this activity is to work with eligible States and motor carrier industry stakeholders to implement expanded CVISN capabilities that improve the safety and productivity of commercial vehicle operations, and enhance transportation security in four primary areas: driver information sharing, enhanced safety information exchange, smart roadside, and expanded electronic credentialing.

R&T PROGRAM NAME: *Enable and Motivate Internal Excellence:* *$1.4M*

- **FMCSA CMV Roadside Technology Corridor.** The objective is to demonstrate and evaluate new CMV safety enforcement technologies in the real-world setting of a fully operational roadside safety inspection and weigh station with truck and bus safety inspectors.
- **FMCSA Program Management.** The objective is to improve the performance and excellence of the Office of Analysis, Research, and Technology (ART), as well as the Agency.
- **TRB/FMCSA Partnerships.** The objective is to broaden participation and utilize expertise of the Transportation Research Board (TRB) in FMCSA safety solutions and ART program evaluation.

ADMINISTRATIVE EXPENSES: *$2M*

		FY 2010 Enacted	FY 2012 Pres. Bud.	FY 2012 Applied	FY 2012 Development
FEDERAL MOTOR CARRIER SAFETY ADMINISTRATION					
Motor Carrier Safety		**11,106**	**11,640**	**6,476**	**814**
A.	**Produce Safe Drivers**	**3,697**	**4,195**	**2,195**	**250**
1.	Produce Safe Drivers	1,997	2,445	2,195	250
2.	Produce Safe Drivers (T)	1,700	1,750	NA	NA
B.	**Improve Safety of Commercial Vehicles**	**1,754**	**1,850**	**200**	**0**
1.	Improve Safety of Commercial Vehicles	0	200	200	0
2.	Improve Safety of Commercial Vehicles (T)	1,754	1,650	NA	NA
C.	**Produce Safer Carriers**	**229**	**1,130**	**980**	**300**
1.	Produce Safer Carriers	229	1,130	980	300
2.	Produce Safer Carriers (T)	0	0	NA	NA
D.	**Advanced Safety Through Info-Based Initiatives**	**1,542**	**450**	**0**	**0**
1.	Advanced Safety Through Info-Based Initiatives	842	0	0	0
2.	Advanced Safety Through Info-Based Initiatives (T)	700	450	NA	NA
E.	**Enable and Motivate Internal Excellence**	**1,321**	**1,375**	**725**	**0**
1.	Enable and Motivate Internal Excellence	1,021	725	725	0
2.	Enable and Motivate Internal Excellence (T)	300	650	NA	NA
F.	**Administrative Expenses**	**2,563**	**2,640**	**2,376**	**264**
	Subtotal, Research & Development	6,652	7,140	6,476	814
	Subtotal, Technology Investment (T)	4,454	4,500		
	Subtotal, Facilities (F)	0	0		
	Total FMCSA	**11,106**	**11,640**	**6,476**	**814**

National Highway Traffic Safety Administration (NHTSA)

NHTSA Research and Analysis

The President's Fiscal Year 2012 budget request for NHTSA is $144.5 million. The $78.2M for Research and Analysis that includes $21.4M for Crashworthiness Research, $12.7M for Crash Avoidance Research, $42.7M for Data Programs and $1.5 M for Alternative Fuels Safety. The request also includes $13.0M for Highway Safety Research and $53.2M for Administrative Expenses.

Research direction and the resulting programs and projects developed are based on the safety needs identified from analysis of crash data as gathered and compiled by the National Center for Statistics and Analysis and other available data. These programs and projects serve to inform agency decision making for promulgation of FMVSS and implementation of Highway Safety Programs, as well as decision making by DOT and sister agencies. These activities are planned and implemented in close coordination with numerous DOT and other governmental agencies.

Crashworthiness Research: $21.4M

- Applied Vehicle Safety Research programs support agency missions in Vehicle Crashworthiness Safety Systems, Alternative Fuel Vehicle Safety and support for CAFE standards. Our Safety Systems research will focus on advanced restraint systems, head restraints, vehicle rollover, child restraints, frontal oblique and corner crash impact protection, motor coach ejections heavy vehicle under-ride, computer modeling of vehicle structures, and related programs. These efforts are coordinated with FHWA, FMCSA, EPA, DOE, and other government agencies.
- Biomechanics research will continue its program to study human injury mechanisms and physical outcomes and develop anthropomorphic test devices (dummies) to support the agency's missions. Key programs include upgrade THOR dummies, develop advanced child dummies, develop the WorldSID dummy, continue CIREN center-based research, specify the detection of hypothermia and countermeasures, complete assessment of Rear Impact dummy responses, continue developing human body finite element models, developing predictive algorithms for serious injury from Advanced Crash Notification (ACN) data, and validate rotational brain injury and multi-point chest injury criteria. These efforts are coordinated efforts with international safety agencies, the automotive industry, DOD, and other government agencies.

Crash Avoidance Research: $12.7M

11

- Crash Avoidance and Pneumatic Tire research includes crash avoidance technologies for light and heavy vehicles, human factors, intelligent vehicle technologies for light and heavy vehicles, and pneumatic tires. Human Factors research will focus on driver distraction, impaired drivers from alcohol and fatigue, pedestrian risks from quiet cars, and related areas. Intelligent technologies will focus on advanced driver assistance and warning systems, vehicle control, and vehicle communications. Electronic Controls reliability and Cybersecurity will be a new and additional area of focus in FY2012. This program also supports agency rulemaking on tires to improve safety and fuel economy. These efforts are coordinated with RITA, FMCSA, FHWA, DOD, and other government agencies.
- Heavy Vehicle Research supports the Agency's rulemaking efforts by improving crash avoidance measures for heavy vehicles including braking, handling, visibility characteristics, mitigating collisions between heavy trucks and other vehicles, and improving driver performance through advanced technologies. We will continue developing test procedures for single unit and bus stability control, forward crash warning systems with active braking, and electronic vision enhancement systems. Additionally these programs support CAFÉ efforts for heavy vehicles. These efforts are coordinated with FMCSA, EPA, and other government agencies.

Data Programs: $42.7M

- Data programs include the Fatality analysis Reporting System (FARS), National Accident Sampling System (NASS), State Data Program, Special Crash Investigation (SCI), Data Analysis Program, Regulatory Analysis and Program Evaluations, and the National Occupant Protection Use Survey and other surveys (e.g. Not in Traffic). These data systems are the backbone of NHTSA's data driven approach to program planning, priority setting, and performance management. These data systems are used by other US DOT modes, the States for their program planning, the automotive industry, and numerous non-governmental organizations interested in traffic safety.

Alternative Fuels Vehicle Safety: $1.5M

- Alternative Fuel Vehicle Safety research addresses the primary safety hazards and failure consequences of alternate fuels including lithium ion batteries, compressed natural gas, and hydrogen fuel cells and related technologies in motor vehicle applications. We will develop test procedures, failure criteria, conduct testing on hybrid and electric vehicles, and identify and evaluate possible mitigation technologies that address hazards from electrical isolation, chemical spill, fire, and explosion during charging and post- crash. These efforts are coordinated efforts with FMCSA, PHMSA, DOE, DOD, NASA, and other government agencies.

Highway Safety Research: $13.0M

- Highway Safety Research directly supports the Department and Agency's goals of reducing traffic crashes, fatalities and injuries by providing the scientific basis for the development of effective countermeasures to reduce the occurrence of traffic crashes.
- Behavioral Safety Research focuses on agency priority issues that contribute significantly to the death, injury, and property damage costs resulting from crashes on our highways.
- These issues include: alcohol and drug impaired driving, occupant protection (seat belt use and child passenger safety), speeding, older driver safety, motorcycle safety, driver licensing, young and novice drivers, driver education, pedestrian and bicycle safety, and other unsafe driving behaviors, such as fatigued, inattentive, and distracted driving. Evaluation research documents the relative effectiveness of programs and is critical to achieving further progress and meeting national goals and performance targets.
- Research, analysis and demonstration program results assess existing and emerging highway safety problems. NHTSA disseminates these results to the States for implementation using the highway safety formula grant (Section 402) funds.

Administrative Expenses: $53.2M

- Administrative expenses cover all operations and maintenance cost associated with the Research, Development and Technology program at NHTSA which does not receive a separate appropriation for this purpose.

RESEARCH, DEVELOPMENT & TECHNOLOGY
DEPARTMENT OF TRANSPORTATION
BUDGET AUTHORITY
(In thousands of dollars)

NATIONAL HIGHWAY TRAFFIC SAFETY ADMINISTRATION	FY 2010 Enacted	FY 2012 Pres. Bud.	FY 2012 Applied	FY 2012 Development
A. Research and Analysis	**60,803**	**78,252**	**35,591**	**0**
1. Crashworthiness	19,226	21,376	21,376	0
a. Safety Systems	8,226	8,376	8,376	0
b. Biomechanics	11,000	13,000	13,000	0
c. Partnership for a New Generation of Vehicles	0	0	0	0
2. Crash Avoidance	10,219	12,715	12,715	0
Driver / Vehicle Performance	8,104	10,500	10,500	0
Heavy Vehicles	2,115	2,215	2,215	0
3. Data programs (T)	26,858	42,661	0	0
Fatal Accident Reporting System (T)	8,472	11,210	NA	NA
National Accident Sampling System (NASS)(T)	12,530	19,686	NA	NA
Data Analysis Program (T)	1,666	2,850	NA	NA
State Data Program (T)	2,490	2,861	NA	NA
Special Crash Investigations (T)	1,700	2,204	NA	NA
Regulatory Analysis/Program Evaluation	0	1,050	NA	NA
National Occupant Protection Use Survey & Other Surveys (T)	0	2,800	NA	NA
6. Alternative Fuels Vehicle Safety (Hydrogen)	4,500	1,500	1,500	0
B. Highway Safety Research	**7,541**	**13,049**	**13,049**	**0**
C. Administrative Expenses	**42,113**	**53,185**	**40,812**	**0**
Administrative Expenses	29,351	40,812	40,812	0
Administrative Expenses (T)	12,762	12,373	NA	NA
Subtotal, Research & Development	**70,837**	**89,452**	**89,452**	**0**
Subtotal, Technology Investment (T)	**39,620**	**55,034**		
Subtotal, Facilities (F)	**0**	**0**		
Total NHTSA	**110,457**	**144,486**	**89,452**	**0**

Federal Railroad Administration (FRA)

The FY2012 budget submission for FRA's Research, Development and Technology is $95.5 million. The core Research & Development (R&D) component is $40 million. This is an increase of approximately $2.4 million over the enacted FY2010 level. The FY2012 submission also includes $50 million for high-speed rail R&D, which is an increase of $20 million from the FY2010 level.

Core Railroad R&D Program: $40M

The core railroad R&D program ($40M) provides science and technology support for FRA's safety rulemaking and enforcement efforts. It also stimulates technological advances in conventional and high-speed railroads. The program focuses on the following areas of research:

- **Railroad systems issues** – research into system safety, performance-based regulations, equipment and infrastructure security, and environmental issues.
- **Human factors** – research to evaluate risks due to human factors related causes to identify, develop and support the introduction of solutions.
- **Rolling stock and components** – research into on-board and wayside monitoring systems, and material and design improvements to address equipment related risks.
- **Track and structures** – research into inspection techniques, material and component reliability, track and structure design and performance, and track stability.
- **Track and train interaction** – research into derailment mechanisms and vehicle-track performance.
- **Train control** – research, testing and evaluation of train control systems.
- **Grade crossings** – research into human factors and infrastructure failure causes of accidents.
- **Hazardous materials transportation** – research into HAZMAT transportation safety, damage assessment and inspection, and improved tank car safety.
- **Train occupant protection** - research into improved locomotive and passenger car safety and crashworthiness.
- **Facilities and test equipment** – support to the Transportation Technology Center (TTC), and the maintenance and operation of inspection cars used for track research and monitoring. TTC is a government-owned facility near Pueblo, Colorado, operated by the Association of American Railroads under a contract for care, custody and control.
- **National Cooperative Rail Research Program (NCRRP)** – enables the FRA to (1) efficiently gather inputs from all stakeholders (e.g. railroads, states,

technology partners and university researchers) in the Nation's rail transportation system to establish research priorities; and (2) accelerate the real-world impact of FRA's R&D by strengthening and broadening the academic and industrial railroad technical communities.

High-Speed Rail R&D: $50M

The high-speed rail R&D program addresses the important safety risks when the density or speed of passenger trains increases, and the new technology that is needed to realize the vision described in the National Rail Plan progress report, September 2010. Examples of key safety-related high-speed rail research needs are interoperability with existing equipment, and more accurate and optimum track components for shared passenger and freight corridors. Examples of new technology needs for high-speed are track-friendly locomotives and higher speed track inspection methods.

The core and high-speed R&D programs strongly support the Department's key **safety** goal. Core research into track, equipment and signaling and train control contributes significantly to the **state of good repair** goal. Track and signaling research makes significant contribution to the **economic competitiveness** goal by demonstrating the performance of domestically manufactured components. Railroad systems research into alternative fuels and lubricants is directed towards the **environmental sustainability** goal. High-speed rail R&D contributes to most of the DOT's strategic goals, including a significant focus on **livable communities**.

The increase in the budget for core R&D compared to the FY2010 enacted level is explained as follows:

- Track research program (additional $1M) – to facilitate the implementation of previously developed technologies for inspecting, analyzing and monitoring the track system; to ensure TTC is ready to test new components arriving on the market; and to fund the new NCRRP.
- Equipment and operating practices program (additional $887k) – to increase the focus on human factors causes of accidents including fatigue and distraction; to accelerate the research into improved crashworthiness of passenger cars; and to advance environmental sustainability technologies.
- Signals, train control and communication program (additional $500k) – to accelerate the development of Positive Train Control technologies to help achieve the 2015 deadline for implementation; and for additional technology demonstrations aimed at increasing grade crossing safety.

The increased budget for high-speed rail R&D ($50M) shown as "Capital Assistance for High Speed Rail") is a direct result of the increased funding requested for the

16

development of high-speed rail corridors. Significant investment is required at TTC to ensure the facility is prepared for testing high-speed rail equipment and components. Domestic suppliers of rail technology and products require stimulus funding to ensure they are ready to meet the demands of the future high-speed rail market.

The Volpe National Transportation System Center is a key partner for FRA and supports many of FRA's R&D projects and initiatives. In addition, there are currently nine universities that receive FRA R&D grants, which also directly support FRA's R&D mission and goals.

RESEARCH, DEVELOPMENT & TECHNOLOGY
DEPARTMENT OF TRANSPORTATION
BUDGET AUTHORITY
(In thousands of dollars)

FEDERAL RAILROAD ADMINISTRATION	FY 2010 Enacted	FY 2012 Pres. Bud.	FY 2012 Applied	FY 2012 Development
A. Railroad Research and Development	37,613	40,000	7,725	29,425
Track Structures				
Track and Structures	5,450	5,450	1,550	3,900
Track and Train Interaction	3,600	3,800	1,200	2,600
R&D Facilities and Test Equipment (F)	2,550	2,850	NA	NA
Rail Cooperative Research Program	0	500	500	0
Equipment and Operating Practices				
Human Factors	3,270	3,670	375	3,295
Rolling Stock and Components	3,000	3,000	300	2,700
Hazardous Materials Transportation	1,550	1,550	250	1,300
Train Occupant Protection	4,600	4,700	1,200	3,500
Railroad Systems Issues	3,623	4,010	1,000	3,010
Signals, Train Control and Communication				
Train Control	7,870	8,270	1,000	7,270
Grade Crossings	2,100	2,200	350	1,850
B. Capital Assistance for High Speed Rail Corridors	30,000	50,000	10,000	40,000
C. Safety and Operations	3,974	5,454	1,200	4,254
1. Salaries and Expenses (R&D)	3,974	5,454	1,200	4,254
Subtotal, Research & Development	69,037	92,604	18,925	73,679
Subtotal, Technology Investment (T)	0	0		
Subtotal, Facilities (F)	2,550	2,850		
Total FRA	71,587	95,454	18,925	73,679

Federal Transit Administration (FTA)

With the FY2012 Budget Submission, FTA has reorganized its programs to mirror a new overall structure that promotes the Administration's priorities for public transportation and that moves forward on a number of FTA reauthorization proposals.

Specifically, the Administration proposes the following Transit Accounts for FY 2012: Transit Formula Grants, Bus and Rail State of Good Repair, Transit Expansion and Livable Communities, Operations and Safety and National Research & Technology Deployment.

With respect specifically to the FTA's National Research & Technology Deployment Account, FTA proposes **$129.2 million** in funding for the following programs in FY 2012.

National Research: $20M
National Research supports efforts in:
- Safety innovation research
- Asset management and maintenance research
- Industry analysis research
- Bus programs research
- Bus testing program
- Rail programs and infrastructure research
- Transit standards development
- International scanning
- Small business innovative research
- Transit planning and forecasting research
- Research to improve the rider experience
- Transit connectivity research, and
- Rural and targeted populations research

Transit Cooperative Research Program: $9.73M which supports research work identified and carried out by consensus of a committee representing the transit industry.

University Transportation Centers Program: $8.0M to support universities for public transportation research, curriculum development, and training.

National Public Transportation Institutes:$5.0M to provide workforce training in planning and service concepts, operation improvements and safety, human resource policies, and management development and effectiveness.

Greenhouse gas and Energy Reduction Deployment and Demonstration Program: $75M

- o Transit Test Beds: $10M. This program will test and demonstrate specific technologies at designated transit agencies. FTA will competitively select two transit agencies to operate "transit test beds" to adapt, test and evaluate new technologies in transit operations and to overcome problems with new technology implementation. This program allows FTA to more immediately and directly assist transit agencies in problem solving and to share implementation lessons nationally.
- o Greenhouse Gas and Energy Reduction Deployment and Demonstration: $65M This large scale deployment program will demonstrate how transit agencies can minimize their energy use as well as the carbon footprint of transit operations.

Clean Fuels and Environmental Research: $14.7M

This research program builds upon efforts previously funded out of the FTA Capital account. This research will focus on advancing vehicle energy management, the electrification of accessories, bus design, rail transit energy management, locomotive design, and alternative fuels. In addition FTA will conduct policy-oriented research on implementation strategies to improve energy efficiency and provide more energy alternatives in transit.

NOTE: A major difference between the FY2010 enacted research budget and the FY2012 proposal is that with FY2012, FTA is seeking to establish a standalone technical assistance activities account distinct from research. The separate program would provide funding for training and capacity building in safety and security, finance and policy, state of good repair, livability, and environmental sustainability for transit agencies and other transit stakeholders. ($34M)

RESEARCH, DEVELOPMENT & TECHNOLOGY
DEPARTMENT OF TRANSPORTATION
BUDGET AUTHORITY
(In thousands of dollars)

FEDERAL TRANSIT ADMINISTRATION		FY 2010 Enacted	FY 2012 Pres. Bud.	FY 2012 Applied	FY 2012 Development
A.	National Program	22,559	20,000	12,500	2,000
	Safety Innovative Research	2,236	2,000	0	2,000
	Bus Program	2,327	2,000	2,000	0
	Bus Testing Program (T)	0	2,000	NA	NA
	Rail Infrastructure Program	2,400	2,000	2,000	0
	Industry Analysis Research	708	500	500	0
	Transit Standards Support	0	0	0	0
	Transit Standards Support (T)	0	1,000	NA	NA
	Asset Mgt & Maintenance Research	5,400	1,000	1,000	0
	Improve Transit Planning and Forcasting	3,725	1,000	1,000	0
	Improve the Rider Experience	780	1,500	1,500	0
	Transit Conductivity Research	1,886	1,500	1,500	0
	Rural and Targeted Populations Research	2,667	2,000	2,000	0
	International Public Transportation Program	0	0	0	0
	International Public Transportation Program (T)	30	500	NA	NA
	Provide Transit Research Leadership	0	0	0	0
	Provide Transit Research Leadership (T)	0	2,000	NA	NA
	Small Business Innovative Research	400	1,000	1,000	0
B.	Technical Assistance and Workforce Development (T)	20,272	0	0	0
C.	Transit Cooperative Research Program (T)	10,000	9,729	NA	NA
D.	National Transit Institute (T)	4,300	0	0	0
E.	University Transportation Centers (T)	7,000	8,000	NA	NA
	Clean Fuels and Environmental Research	1,569	14,743	14,743	0
1.	Clean Fuel and Electric Drive Research	1,469	13,743	13,743	0
2.	Reduce Transit Environmental Impacts	100	1,000	1,000	0
	Greenhouse Gas & Energy Redctn. Deployment & Demo (T)	0	75,000	NA	NA
F.	Subtotal, Greenhouse Gas & Energy Reduction	1,569	89,743	14,743	0
G.	Administrative Expenses	1,051	1,812	1,312	500
	Subtotal, Research & Development	25,149	31,055	28,555	2,500
	Subtotal, Technology Investment (T)	41,602	98,229		
	Subtotal, Facilities (F)	0	0		
	Total FTA	66,751	129,284	28,555	2,500

Federal Highway Administration (FHWA)

Research, Technology & Education (RT&E) Program
FY 2012 Budget Request Overview

Overview

For FY 2012, the FHWA is requesting $951 million. Of this amount, $384 million is for FHWA's core RT&E program, $257 million is for programs administered by the Research and Innovative Technology Administration (RITA), and the remaining $310 million includes such items as $206 million for the State Planning and Research Program and $100 million for the Intelligent Transportation Systems (ITS) Wireless Innovation Fund (WIN) Initiative, which are funded outside of the SAFETEA-LU Title V.

This request will enable FHWA to address current issues, emerging challenges and provide information for policy decisions. The program will conduct, sponsor, sustain, and guide highway research to develop and deliver innovation.

FHWA RT&E Program

Highway Research & Development Program (HRD): $200M

Conduct research and development activities associated with safety, infrastructure preservation, environmental mitigation and streamlining, operations, livability, innovative program delivery solutions, and policy. Although there are requests for funds related to each of 6 major program areas, programming of funds will be guided by multi-year roadmaps that establish research and development priorities.

- Safety: $25M
  - Research focuses on research and development activities aimed at supporting comprehensive and sustainable safety programs.
- Infrastructure: $75M
  - FHWA conducts problem-focused research, development, and communications outreach activities to preserve the existing investment in our Nation's highway infrastructure and to build for the future through the application of advanced technologies that improve infrastructure integrity.
- Planning & Environment: $35M
  - Activities in this program area include carrying out short and long-term livability initiatives to improve project delivery and enhance communities that are impacted by surface transportation projects; developing comprehensive strategies to minimize the impact of transportation

investment on the environment; and adjusting to changing climate conditions.

- Operations: $25M
  - ○ Conduct research on the application of cutting-edge technologies to move people and goods better, quicker, and safer.

  Policy: $18M

  - ○ Conduct analysis on emerging issues, such as climate change, public-private partnerships, highway revenues, performance measurement, and authorization. Policy initiatives include the International Highway Transportation Outreach Program
- Next Generation Research & Technology: $22M
  - ○ Lead a nationally-coordinated highway research and technology program; operate the Turner-Fairbank Highway Research Center as the Federally-owned leader in Highway innovation; and conduct longer-term, higher-risk research with the potential for dramatic breakthroughs in surface transportation.

Technology & Innovation Deployment Program (TIDP): $144M

Conduct testing, evaluating, and accelerating the delivery and deployment of technologies. This program includes deployment activities for Future Strategic Highway Research Program (SHRP 2) implementation, Highways for LIFE, Every Day Counts, and deployment and delivery of innovations developed through the HRD program. Unlike the HRD program, there are no program-area allotments. The TIDP is designed specifically to enable FHWA to more aggressively fill the critical need to turn research products into proven technologies or demonstrate practices, identify the market forces that will influence successful technology and innovation deployment, and plan and deliver effective communication to promote rapid adoption of proven, market-ready technologies and innovations to States, local jurisdictions, and industry.

Training & Education Program (T&E): $40M

Train the current and future transportation workforce; transferring knowledge quickly and effectively. This includes the National Highway Institute, Local/Tribal technical Assistance Programs, Dwight David Eisenhower Transportation Fellowship Program, and the Garret Morgan Technology and Transportation Futures Program. T&E also includes a new initiative, the Surface Transportation Workforce Development Centers Program, which will establish five Centers at institutions of higher education.

Related Programs

State Planning and Research Program (SP&R) Part II: $206.4M

With the reconfiguration of Federal-aid formula programs presented in this budget, funding for this program would come from a 2% set-aside from state apportionments for the Highway Infrastructure Performance Program, the Flexible Investment Program, the Highway Safety Improvement Program, and the Livable Communities Program. States must allocate a minimum of 25 percent of their SP&R apportionment for research, development, and technology (SP&R Part II). SP&R Part II activities involve research on new areas of knowledge; adapting findings to practical applications by developing new technologies; and the transfer of these technologies, including the process of dissemination, demonstration, training, and adoption of innovations by users. The SP&R program is intended to solve problems identified by the states.

Surface Transportation Revenue Alternatives Office: $20M

The proposed office will lead a phased research and demonstration effort to analyze a range of revenue-generation alternatives with the potential to replace the petroleum-based system currently used to fund surface transportation programs. The office, guided by a Policy Decision Group consisting of a wide range of stakeholders, will deliver a program that includes a broad agenda of research, outreach, system design and field trials. The program will develop a study framework defining the desired functionality of preferred alternative revenue generation systems, as well as a communications effort designed to increase public and stakeholder awareness and understanding regarding the relevant issues. In addition, it will include the development of a concept of operations for the preferred scheme(s) and development of high-level system architectures, interoperability standards and communication protocols, and equipment standards. Field trials to demonstrate and test the capabilities of interest will also be covered under this program.

Crosswalk of Consolidated Highway Programs*

Interstate Maintenance
Highway Bridge Program
National Highway System
Territorial Highway Program (NHS Set-aside)
Alaska Highway (NHS Set-aside)
Surface Transportation Program
Ferry Boat Program
Appalachian Development Highway System
Equity Bonus
Revenue Aligned Budget Authority
Puerto Rico Highway Program
Denali Access System Program
Delta Region Transportation Development Program
Metropolitan Planning
Lake Tahoe Planning
Statewide Planning & Research (SP&R)

National Highway Program:

- Highway Infrastructure Performance Program (HIPP)
- Flexible Investment Program
- Territorial Highway Program (HIPP Set-aside)
- SP&R and Metro Planning continue as set-asides from multiple apportioned programs.

Highway Safety Improvement Program
Hazard Elimination at High-Speed Rail Highway Crossings
Railway-Highway Crossings
High Risk Rural Roads
Operation Lifesaver
Work Zone Safety Grants
National Work Zone Safety Clearinghouse
Road Safety (Data & Public Awareness)

Safety Program:

- Highway Safety Improvement Program
- Rural Road Safety Setaside from HSIP
- Highway Safety Data Improvement Program

Congestion Mitigation & Air Quality (CMAQ)
Transportation Enhancements (STP Set-aside)
Recreational Trails
Scenic Byways
America's Byways Resource Center
Safe Routes to School
Transportation, Community & System Preservation
Non-Motorized Pilot Program
Historic Covered Bridge Preservation
Bicycle & Pedestrian Clearinghouse

Livability Program:

- Livable Communities Program
- Investments for Livable Communities Grant Program
- Livability Capacity Building Grant Program

Highways for LIFE
Surface Transp. Research, Development, & Deployment
Training & Education
Future Strategic Highway Research (Set-aside from Apportioned Programs)
Intelligent Transportation Systems (ITS) Research
Great Lakes ITS Implementation
University Transportation Research
Bureau of Transportation Statistics (BTS)

Research, Technology & Education Program:

- Highway Research & Development
- Technology & Innovation Deployment
- Training & Education
- ITS Research (RITA)
- Competitive UTC Consortia (RITA)
- Bureau of Transportation Statistics (RITA)
- Multimodal Innovative Research Program (RITA)

Emergency Relief
Indian Reservation Roads
Indian Reservation Road Bridges
Additional CA for States with Indian Reservations
Park Roads & Parkways
Refuge Roads
Public Lands Highways Discretionary
Public Lands Highways, Forest Highways
Going-to-the-Sun Road, Glacier National Park, Montana
On-the-Job Training (OJT) & Supportive Services
Disadvantaged Business Enterprise (DBE) Training
Grant Program to Prohibit Racial Profiling**
Highway Use Tax Evasion**

Federal Allocation Program:

- Emergency Relief
- Federal Lands Transportation Program
- Federal Lands Access Program
- Tribal Transportation Program
- Workforce Development
  - OJT & Supportive Services
  - DBE Training

National Corridor Infrastructure Program
Coordinated Border Infrastructure Program
Projects of Regional and National Significance
High Priority Projects
Transportation Projects
Interstate Maintenance Discretionary (deduction from IM)
Bridge Set-aside (deduction from Bridge)
Magnetic Levitation Program
Truck Parking Facilities
Freight Intermodal Distribution Pilot Grants
Value Pricing Pilot Program
Pavement Marking Systems Demonstration Projects in Alaska & Tenn.
Road User Fees Field Test – Public Policy Center of Univ. of Iowa
Multimodal Facility Improvements
TIFIA

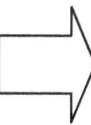

Other:

- Elements of these programs may be included in the I-Bank, Transportation Leadership Award program, core FHWA programs and/or other DOT programs

* Not every eligibility under an old program is continued in a new program.
** No comparable eligibility in new program structure.

	RESEARCH, DEVELOPMENT & TECHNOLOGY DEPARTMENT OF TRANSPORTATION Budget Authority (in thousands of dollars)	FY 2010 Enacted	FY 2012 Pres. Bud.	FY 2012 Applied	FY 2012 Development
	FEDERAL HIGHWAY ADMINISTRATION Research, Technology & Education Program				
(A)	Surface Transp. Research, Development & Deployment	183,634			
A.	Highway Research and Development 1/	183,634	200,000	176,000	24,000
	Safety:	**14,609**	**25,000**	**22,000**	**3,000**
	Safety	7,491			
	Safety (T)	7,118			
	Infrastructure:	**71,266**	**75,000**	**66,000**	**9,000**
	Pavements	33,069			
	Pavements (T)	1,316			
	Structures	26,340			
	Structures (T)	1,079			
	Long-Term Pavement Performance	8,834			
	Long-Term Pavement Performance (T)	628			
	Planning and Environment	**20,921**	**35,000**	**30,800**	**4,200**
	Planning, Environment, and Realty	18,684			
	Planning, Environment, and Realty (T)	2,237			
	Operations (Highway Operations):	**8,999**	**25,000**	**22,000**	**3,000**
	Highway Operations	6,405			
	Highway Operations (T)	2,594			
	Policy:	**1,215**	**18,000**	**15,840**	**2,160**
	International Outreach	1,215			
	Next Generation Research & Technology (Corporate):	**35,418**	**22,000**	**19,360**	**2,640**
	Exploratory Advanced Research	12,221			
	Exploratory Advanced Research (T)	869			
	Corporate R&T	20,845			
	Corporate R&T (T)	1,483			
	Modal Research:	**31,206**	**0**	**0**	**0**
	OST, RITA, FMCSA, NHTSA & PHMSA	31,206			
	OST, RITA, FMCSA, NHTSA & PHMSA (T)				
B.	Technology and Innovation Deployment Program (T) 1/	0	144,000	0	0
(B)	Future Strategic Highway Research Program-SHRP II 1/	49,095	0	0	0
	Future Strategic Highway Research Program-SHRP II	31,912			
	Future Strategic Highway Research Program-SHRP II (T)	17,183			
C.	Surface Transportation Revenue Alternatives Office	0	20,000	2,000	16,000
	Surface Transportation Revenue Alternatives Office		18,000		
	Surface Transportation Revenue Alternatives Office (T)		2,000		
D.	Training and Education	24,965	40,000	0	0
	National Highway Institute (T)	8,668	14,000		
	Local Technical Assistance Program (T)	10,022	16,000		
	Eisenhower Transportation Fellowship Program (T)	1,129	2,750		
	Garrett Morgan Program (T)	1,693	1,250		
	Transportation Education Development Pilot (T)	790	2,075		
	Freight Planning Capacity Building (T)	1,986	900		
	Surface Transportation Congestion Relief Assistance Program (T)	677	775		
	Surface Transportation Workforce Development Centers (T)	0	2,250		

		FY 2010 Enacted	FY 2012 Pres. Bud.	FY 2012 Applied	FY 2012 Development
E.	**Intelligent Transportation System Wireless Initiative (WIN)**	**0**	**100,000**	**0**	**0**
	National Wireless Initiative (WIN)(T)	0	100,000	0	0
F.	**Intelligent Transportation Systems 4/**	**102,850**	**110,000**	**96,100**	**0**
	ITS Multi-modal Research - Applications:	34,809	66,221	66,221	
	ITS Multi-modal Research Technology:	12,325	11,175	11,175	
	ITS Multi-modal Research Policy:	3,053	4,000	4,000	
	Mode Specific Research:	2,109	4,500	4,500	
	Exploratory Research:	550	2,000	2,000	
	Other ITS Research:	28,022	2,704	2,704	
	Technology Transfer and Evaluation:	14,702	13,900		
	ITS Program Support:	7,280	5,500	5,500	
G.	**Competitive University Transportation Center (UTC)**	**73,772**	**72,000**	**0**	**0**
	1. University Transportation Research (T)	73,772	72,000		
H.	**Multimodal Innovative Research Program 4/**	**0**	**20,000**	**10,000**	**10,000**
	Multimodal Research and Technology	0	20,000	10,000	10,000
	Multimodal Research and Technology (T)	0			
I.	**UTC Multimodal Competitive Research Grants 4/**	**0**	**20,000**	**10,000**	**10,000**
	UTC Competive Research Grants	0	20,000	10,000	10,000
	UTC Competitive Research Grants(T)	0			
J.	**State Planning and Research (SPR) 2/**	**182,985**	**206,398**	**156,202**	**21,300**
	1. State Planning and Research (SPR)	157,367	177,502	156,202	21,300
	2. State Planning and Research (SPR) (T)	25,618	28,896		
K.	**Administrative Expenses**	**18,740**	**18,932**	**14,327**	**1,954**
	1. Administrative Expenses	16,116	16,281	14,327	1,954
	2. Administrative Expenses (T)	2,624	2,651		
	Subtotal, Research and Development	453,048	547,883	464,629	83,254
	Subtotal, Technology Investment (T)	182,992	403,447		
	Subtotal RD&T Programs	**636,040**	**951,330**	**464,629**	**83,254**
	Add: Bureau of Transportation Statistics	27,000	35,000		
	Less: Adjustment of BTS Obligation Authority to Contract Authority				
	Less: Adjustment of Contract Authority to Obligation Authority				
	Less: Administrative Expenses	-18,740	-18,932		
	Less: State Planning and Research (SPR)	-182,985	-206,398		
	Less: Future Strategic Highway Research Program-SHRP II	-49,095			
	Less: Surface Transportation Revenue Alternatives Office		-20,000		
	Less: Intelligent Transportation Systems National Wireless Initiative (WIN)		-100,000		
	Total Title V Programs 3/	**412,220**	**641,000**		

Footnotes:

1/ All Highway Research and Development (HRD) Technology or "T" programs are now funded from the Technology and Innovation Deployment Program (TIDP). The TIDP also includes funding for the Future Strategic Highway Research Program (SHRP 2), which was shown separately in previous budget requests, and Highways for Life-type activities. SAFETEA-LU program categories are in paranthesis

2/ Title 23 USC 505(b) requires State DOT's to expend no less than 25 percent of their annual SPR funds on RD&T activities. Total SPR funding represents 2 percent of apportioned programs.

3/ In the absence of authorizing legislation for the Federal-aid Highway Program in FY 2012, the amounts in the exhibit are only estimates.

4/ Details for this program are contained in the Research and Innovative Technology Administration (RITA) FY 2012 budget.

Research and Innovative Technology Administration (RITA)

The President's FY2012 budget includes $6.8 million for RITA-administered research, development and technology. RITA also manages $8 million from FTA, and $322 million from FHWA.

Alternative Fuels R&D: $0.5M

- To fulfill its role as DOT's lead agency in support of Alternative Fuels R&D, RITA will continue to coordinate, manage and execute key components of the Department's alternative fuels activities in collaboration with DOT Operating Administrations, DOE, EPA, USDA, Federal, State, academic, and industry partners. This includes participating with the congressionally-mandated Biomass Research and Development Board, hosting the Interagency Biofuels Infrastructure workshop April 2011, and facilitating intermodal and cross-cutting innovative research through the DOT Alternative Fuels Working Group.

Research, Development and Technology (RD&T) Coordination: $ 0.9M

- RITA is carrying out the Mineta Act mandate to ensure RD&T coordination and collaboration and leveraging of resources within DOT and with external entities.
- SAFETEA-LU required a DOT R&D Strategic Plan and a review by the National Academies' National Research Council (NRC). Using the DOT Strategic Plan as a guiding document, the DOT RD&T Planning Team developed the **2011 – 2016 DOT RD&T Strategic Plan.** The Plan will be published this spring in the Federal Register through which comments and suggestions will be solicited from the public. The public's comments and suggestions will be reviewed and incorporated into the plan as deemed appropriate by the RDT Planning Team and an expert panel led by the chairman of the original NRC review committee. The finalized 2011-2016 DOT RD&T Strategic Plan will be published this summer.
- During the past 12 months, RITA formed 14 **Research Clusters** composed of DOT researchers and faculty from DOT-funded universities to communicate through a SharePoint site for information sharing and research collaboration. Support is needed in 2012 to continue and maintain this effort, to enhance the use of social media for information dissemination and to host virtual and in-person research seminars and critical topic reviews.
- Also during the past 12 months, RITA initiated a Transportation **Technology Transfer** program supportive of transportation product development and dissemination to enhance the Department's ability to identify and support technology transfer of products of University Research Centers. RITA is

sponsoring the first annual University Transportation Center (UTC) Technology Transfer Showcase on Wednesday, April 6 at US DOT headquarters, highlighting the work of 25 UTCs.

- To enhance awareness and transparency, RITA has developed a web-based **Knowledge Management System** in response to a GAO recommendation that RITA develop a searchable database for R&D activities. The objective of this initiative is to maintain a repository that fully integrates information about R&D at the project level funded by DOT, both internally at DOT and externally at universities. Additional FY 2012 funding will support the posting and maintenance of the database as well as data mining to develop composite reports of DOT research in key areas, identification of new cluster areas, and identification of research products for technology transfer.

Positioning, Navigation and Timing: $1M

- The Positioning, Navigation and Timing Program (PNT) coordinates DOT PNT technology and policy, as well as provides civil PNT systems analysis which is critical to intermodal transportation applications. In 2007, the Secretary of Transportation delegated the DOT PNT responsibility to RITA.
- Per **National Security Presidential Directive-39**, DOT serves as the lead for PNT requirements, architecture development, and GPS acquisition, development, and operations for all United States Government civil departments and agencies.
- The PNT Program is essential to ensuring that critical infrastructures have the primary and back-up PNT systems upon which they depend for daily operations, as well as identifying and pursuing gaps and research needed to meet these requirements, to enable future systems such as NextGen, Positive Train Control, and Intelligent Transportation Systems (ITS).
- During the past 12 months, DOT and DoD, in conjunction with 29 other government departments and agencies and outreach to industry and universities, completed the **National PNT Architecture Implementation Plan**. This plan provides a roadmap through 2025 to overcome capability gaps predominantly resulting from the limitations of GPS.
- The PNT program produces the **Federal Radionavigation Plan** in conjunction with DoD and DHS, the Civil PNT Requirements Document, chairs the Civil GPS Service Interface Committee, and advances the National PNT Architecture in conjunction with the Department of Defense and other government agencies

Competitive University Transportation Centers (UTC) Program [$100M]*

- *The funding will come through FHWA ($92M) and FTA ($8M) to RITA.

- The UTC Program will consist of two components: A. base funding of $80M for multimodal and multidisciplinary UTC consortia around particular theme areas, plus B. an additional $20M that will be reserved for a targeted multimodal research program for which the UTCs can compete. By funding university research and education, the USDOT is investing in our nation's intellectual transportation capacity.

A. Competitive UTC Consortia [$80M]*

- o *The funding will come through FHWA ($72M) and FTA ($8M) to RITA.
- o The UTC Program was initiated in 1987 under the Surface Transportation and Uniform Relocation Assistance Act, which authorized the establishment and operation of transportation centers in each of the 10 standard federal regions. The Program was reauthorized and expanded in 1991, 1998, and 2005. In 2005, SAFETEA-LU reauthorized the Program, increasing the number of Centers from 33 to 60. In addition to the 10 Regional Centers, which were competitively selected, 10 Tier-1-funded Centers were competitively selected. All of the UTCs except for the Title III Centers are required to have a one-for-one funding match. The current legislation does not require the Title III centers to match their grant funding dollar for dollar. The 60 Centers include a total of 125 universities. The UTC grants support research, education and technology transfer.
- o The UTC Program's mission is to advance transportation expertise and technology in the many disciplines that comprise transportation through education, research and technology transfer at university-based consortia.
- o The UTC Program provides a critical transportation knowledge base outside of the USDOT and addresses critical workforce needs for future generations of transportation leaders. USDOT proposes to reform the UTC Program by competitively selecting UTC consortia that will be governed by peer review principles. All UTCs will be selected via rigorous competition that will include incentives for addressing key USDOT priorities.
- o Each competitively selected UTC consortia will receive baseline funding. These competitively selected recipients will also be eligible to receive funds from the UTC Multimodal Competitive Research Grants.

- **B. UTC Multimodal Competitive Research Grants: [$20M]***
  - o *The funding will come through FHWA to RITA.
  - o Most USDOT research is funded on a mode-by-mode basis. In order to encourage cross-modal research, the Secretary will appoint an internal cross-modal USDOT governance council to select annual priorities for

targeted research needs. The University Transportation Center (UTC) Competitive Research Grant Program reserves 20 percent of the total $100M competitive UTC program to provide USDOT's modal administrations access to the nation's top academic researchers and University-based laboratories to *address specific cross-modal research priorities* in the areas of safety, state of good repair, economic competitiveness, livable communities and environmental sustainability.

- o This program will allow all modal administrations to bring research needs, unanticipated issues, and quick-response problems to the table on an annual basis that UTC universities can compete for. This unique cross-modal program *will enable USDOT staff to engage directly in partnership with UTC researchers to solve pressing problems or support policy decisions on a more nimble and responsive basis.* Eligible recipients of these grants will be any of the universities participating in the competitively selected UTCs.

- o Frequently, UTCs develop promising results in their outlined baseline funded programs that modal administrations wish to capitalize on or to more specifically focus. These funds will allow modal administrations to develop Statements of Work to obtain that follow-on research to answer specific questions or to tap into unique expertise developed by a particular UTC consortium.

*Multimodal Innovative Research Program: [$20M]**

- • *The funding will come through FHWA to RITA. The Multimodal Innovative Research Program is a restructuring of the current Advanced Research Program, managed by RITA. The existing Advanced Research Program is a reimbursable program with FHWA that funds research relevant to FHWA but also applicable to other modal administrations.

- • Using the DOT RD&T Planning Team and RD&T Planning Council as cross-modal selecting bodies, the new program will fund a set of collaboratively outlined long-term research priorities. Competitively solicited proposals for the research will be open to bid by industry, university or state-based stakeholders and will serve as the basis for this Departmental, multi-modal research agenda. Guided by the **USDOT RD&T Strategic Plan**, this initiative will create opportunities for funding cross-modal research that is aimed at solving transportation problems at the interfaces between modes, or problems that affect more than one mode.

- • The initiative will also include a component fostering creativity and innovation that can support a competition and prize program aimed at solving urgent transportation problems, in support of the Administration's Open Government initiative. This program will also support key partnerships with other Federal agencies to fully leverage their investments in transportation research and product development to address transportation issues.

- The program will competitively award contracts for advanced multimodal transportation research to facilitate practical innovative approaches to solve transportation problems related to attainment of USDOT strategic goals and multi-modal elements of the *DOT RD&T Strategic Plan*; to address issues affecting policy, and cross-modal concerns such as efficient and intermodal goods and passenger movements; and to support development of advanced vehicle technologies and application/repurposing of existing technologies such as remote sensing and spatial information products.

- Research products and results from this initiative will provide: 1. Transportation system applications of advanced transportation technologies, methodologies, policies and decisions; 2. Best practices in planning, operations, design and maintenance of transportation and related systems; 3. Technology identification, modification and dissemination through outreach to other federal agencies, state and local transportation agencies and other public, private and academic stakeholders in the industry.

- Successful projects will support U.S. DOT strategic goals by applying state-of-the art advanced technology solutions to multimodal transportation issues. The program will focus on research to result in 'quick turnaround' products – applied vs. basic technology development including methodologies, policy guidelines, planning tools, prototypes/pilot products for practical application.

*Intelligent Transportation Systems: Core Program [$110M]**

- *ITS Program funding and administrative support comes from FHWA, and the RITA Administrator provides the strategic direction for the Program.

- The ITS Program dates back over the past three surface authorizations and is specifically authorized under Section 5301 of SAFETEA-LU. It calls for a broad range of multi-modal ITS research activities to address surface related improvements in transportation safety, mobility, and environmental benefits. In addition to the core research mission, the ITS program is also authorized to address the development of standards and architecture, expansion of road weather data and systems integration, professional workforce development (i.e training), implementation of a national 511 traveler information system, and technology transfer activities.

- The ITS Program is governed through the ITS Management Council that consists of the Modal Administrators from RITA, FHWA, NHTSA, FMCSA, FTA, FRA and MARAD with Deputy Secretary as chair. With the movement of the ITS JPO into RITA per the Mineta Act, the Deputy Secretary has delegated chair responsibilities to the RITA Administrator. This governance structure ensures that the ITS research program has a multi-modal and cross-modal perspective.

- The *Intelligent Transportation Systems (ITS) Strategic Research Plan, 2010 - 2014* is being implemented to leverage the power of wireless communication to advance transportation safety, mobility and environmental sustainability.

- **Connected Vehicle Research** is wireless communication technology applied to transportation. Specifically this applies to vehicles of all types (cars, trucks and buses), infrastructure and pedestrians. This technology has the potential to prevent cars from crashing, and to reduce congestion on our highways and roads. This is done by sending messages between vehicles, infrastructure, pedestrians, and bicyclists and using that data to manage the entire transportation network more safely and efficiently.

Wireless Innovation (WIN) Fund Initiative [$100M]

- The **Wireless Innovation (WIN) Fund Initiative** is separate from the core ITS research program, and is part of a government-wide initiative to support the President's National Broadband Plan.

  FCC spectrum auctions planned over the next ten years are estimated to produce $27 billion in revenue. The President's Budget requests that $3 billion of the proceeds from these auctions be used across multiple Federal agencies for various wireless broadband applications and infrastructure investments. The ITS program will receive $100M (to be used over a five year period) to help foster new wireless technologies and applications in transportation. Examples of potential applications include wireless "fast lanes" for vehicle inspections, and competitively-selected regional/corridor "test bed" demonstrations of wireless applications for safety, mobility, emergency response, energy, and environmental applications.

RESEARCH, DEVELOPMENT & TECHNOLOGY
DEPARTMENT OF TRANSPORTATION
BUDGET AUTHORITY
(In thousands of dollars)

RESEARCH AND INNOVATIVE TECHNOLOGY ADMINISTRATION	FY 2010 Enacted	FY 2012 Pres. Bud.	FY 2012 Applied	FY 2012 Development
Research and Development				
Salaries and Administrative Expenses	4,701	4,385	3,288	1,097
Alternative Fuels Research & Development	500	500	200	300
R&DT Coordination	536	900	657	243
Positioning, Navigation, and Timing	400	1,000	330	670
University Transportation Research (FHWA)	[73,772]	[72,000]	[0]	[0]
University Transportation Research (FTA)	[7,000]	[8,000]	[0]	[0]
UTC Multimodal Competitive Research Grants	[0]	[20,000]	[10,000]	[10,000]
Multimodal Research and Technology	[0]	[20,000]	[10,000]	[10,000]
Intelligent Transportation Systems: Core Program	[102,850]	[110,000]	[96,100]	[0]
Intelligent Transportation Systems: Wireless Initiative	[0]	[100,000]	[0]	[0]
Total RITA:	**6,137**	**6,785**	**4,475**	**2,310**